I0478691

JORDAN

PHOTOGRAPHS BY ELIZABETH KRAMER

THIS IS PART OF THE VISITING SERIES.

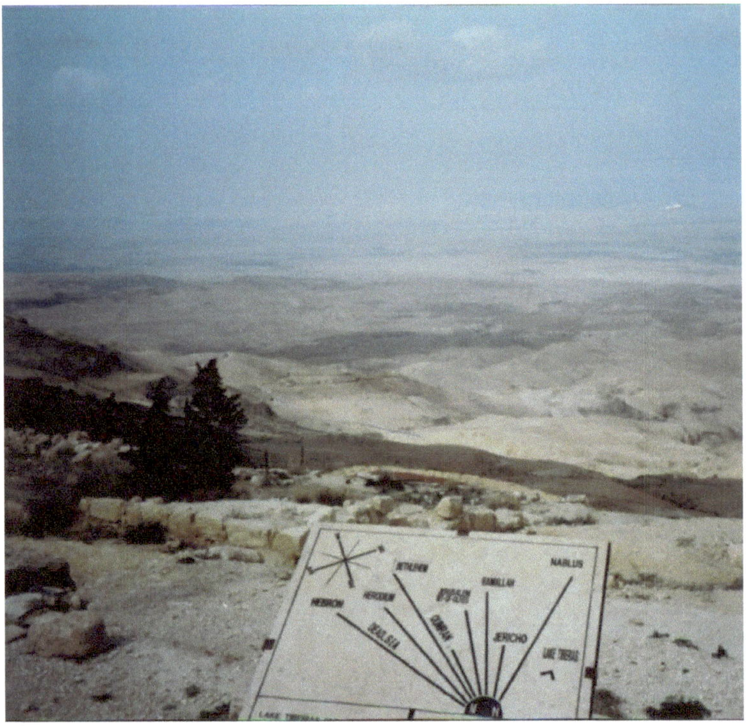
HEBRON
NABLUS
JERICHO

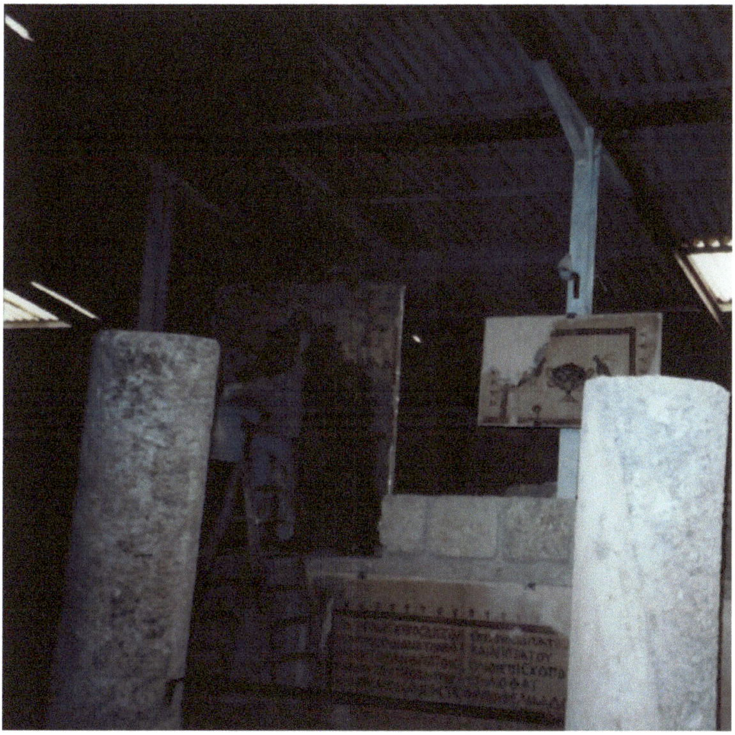

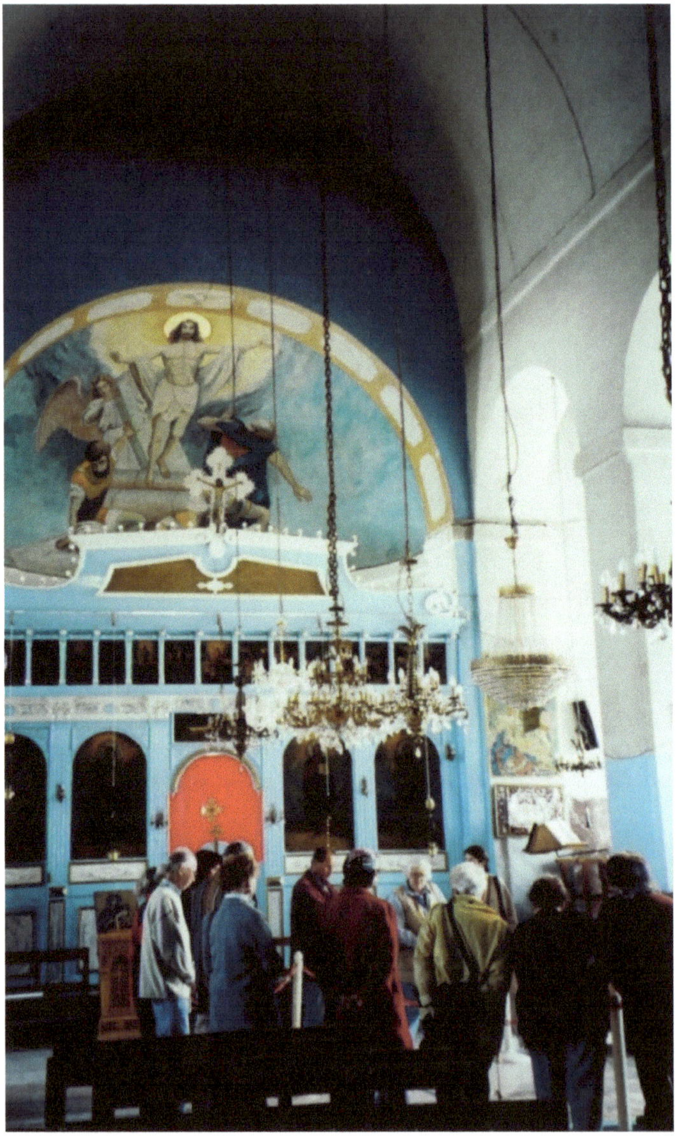

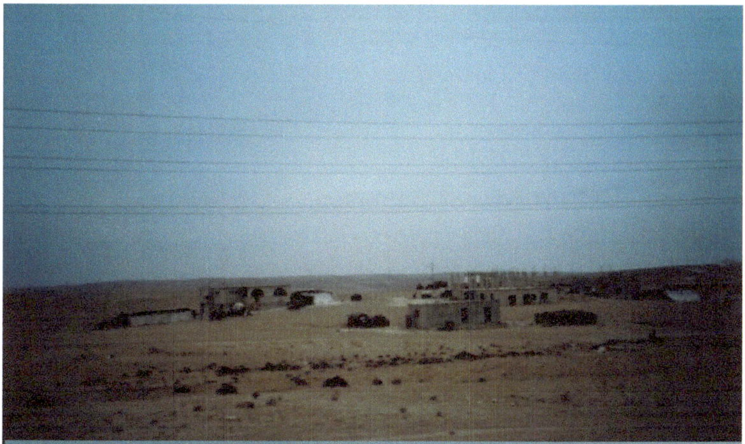

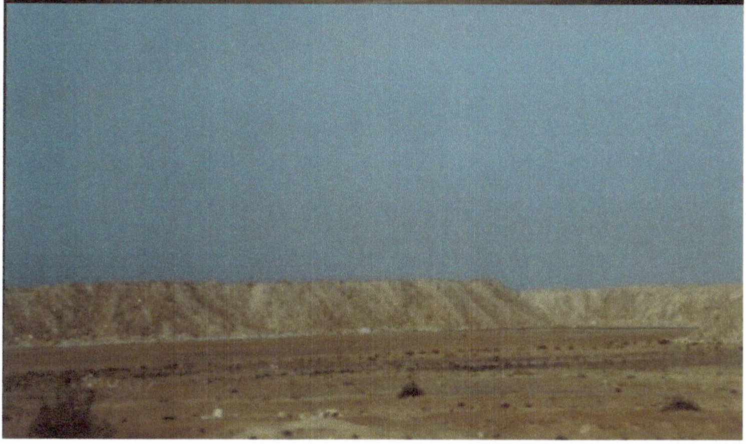

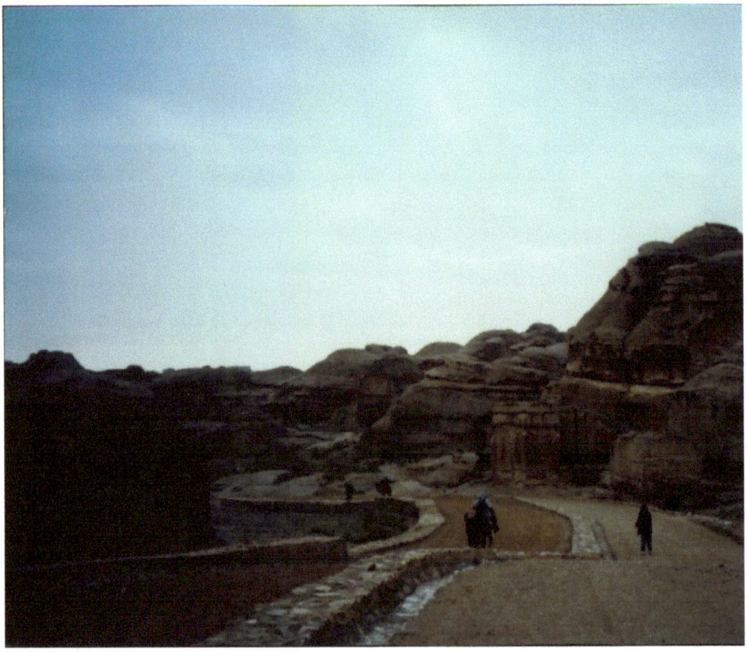

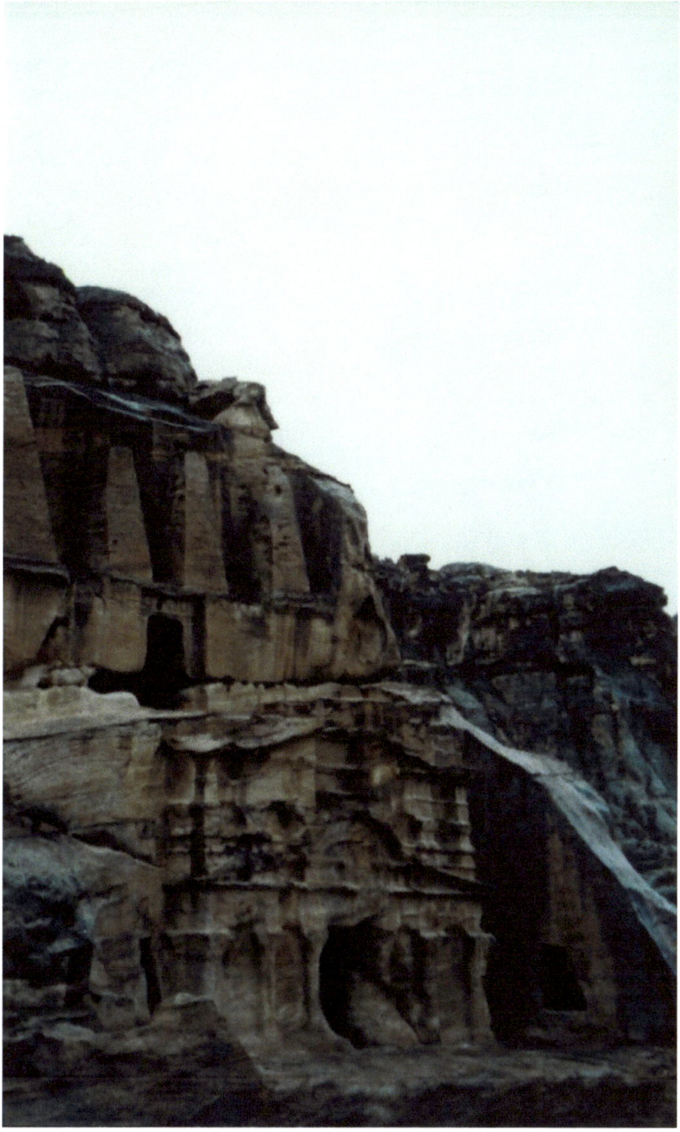

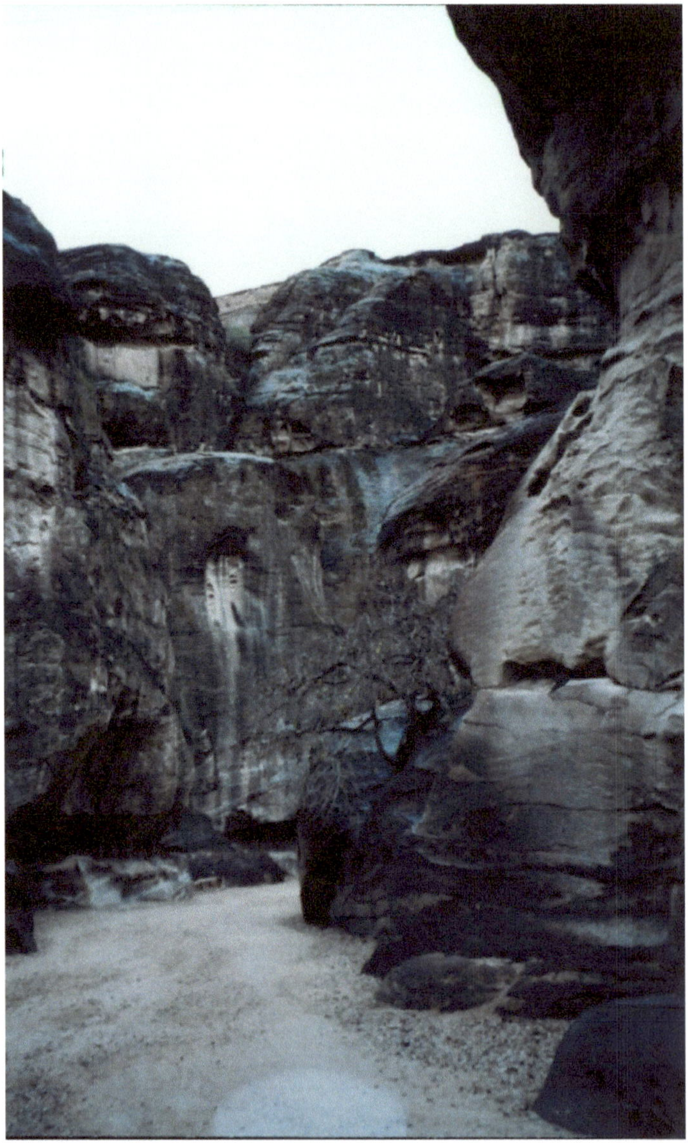

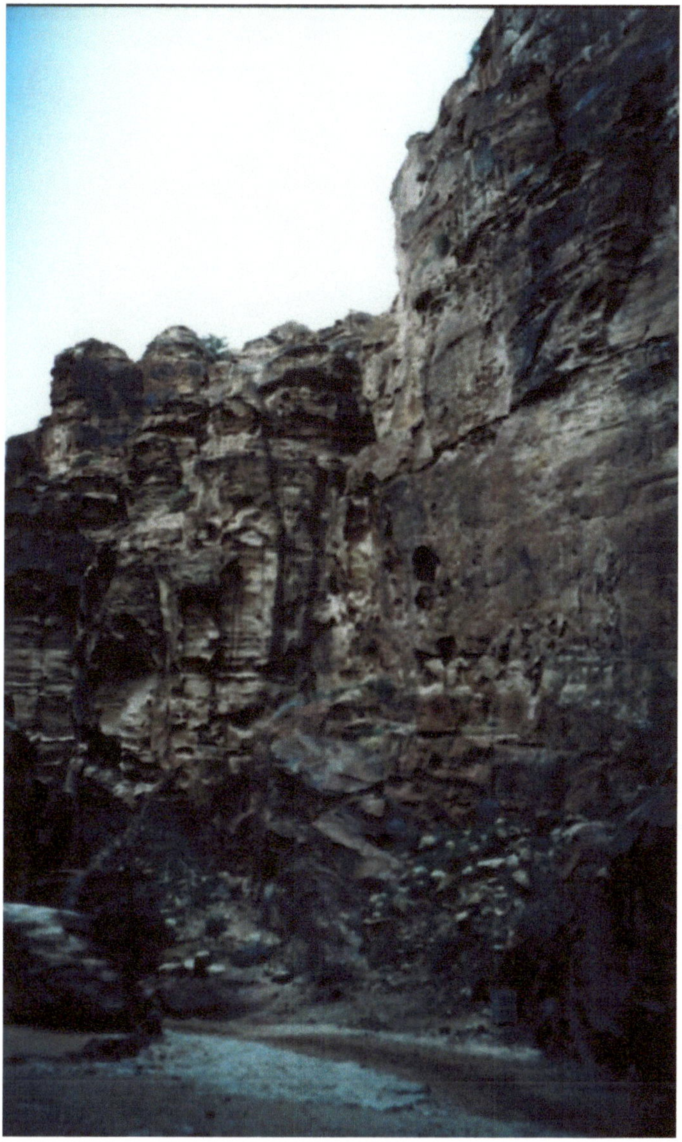

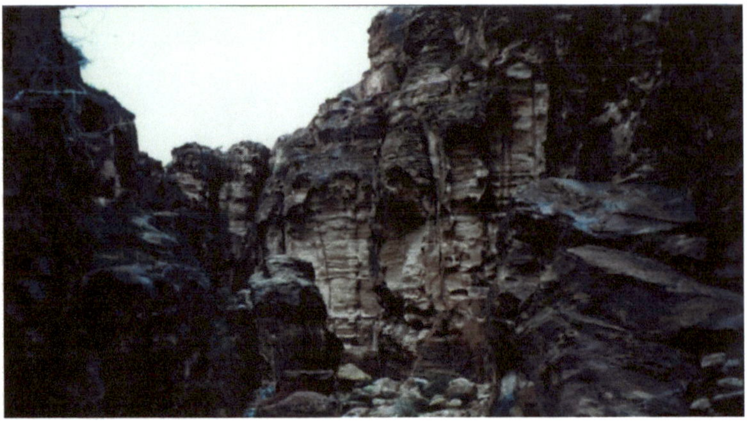

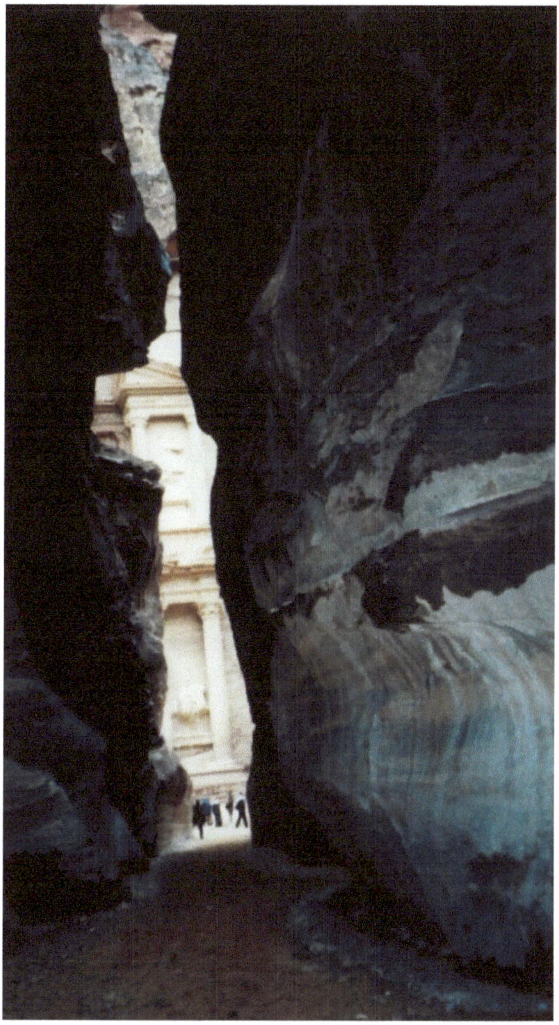

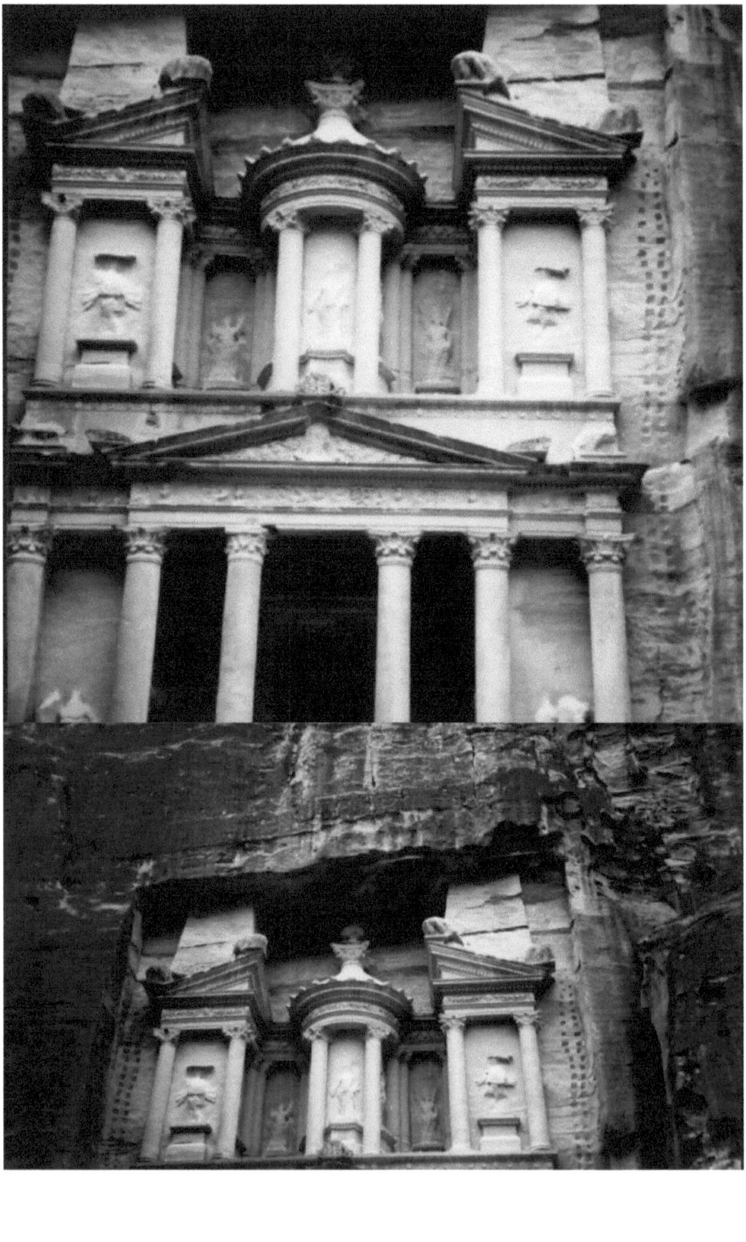

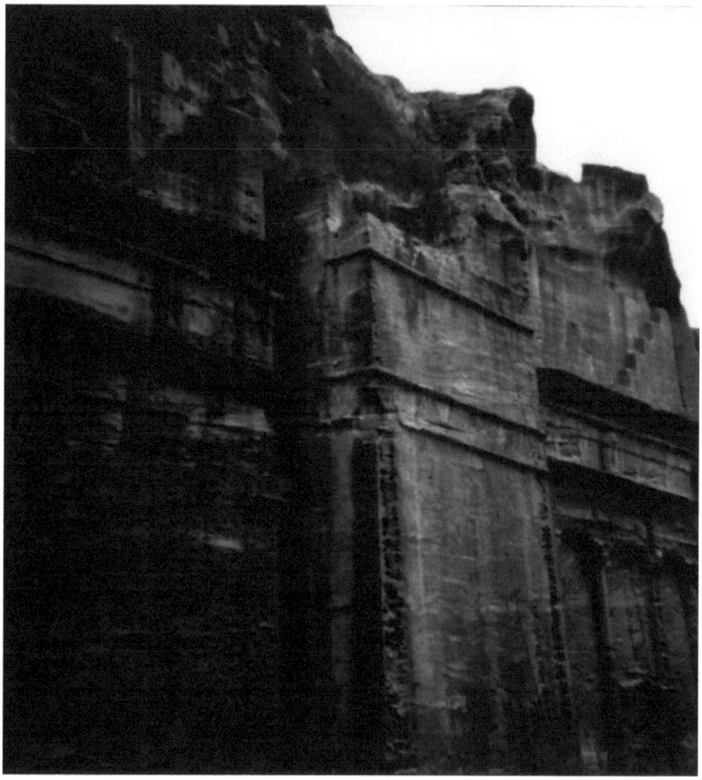

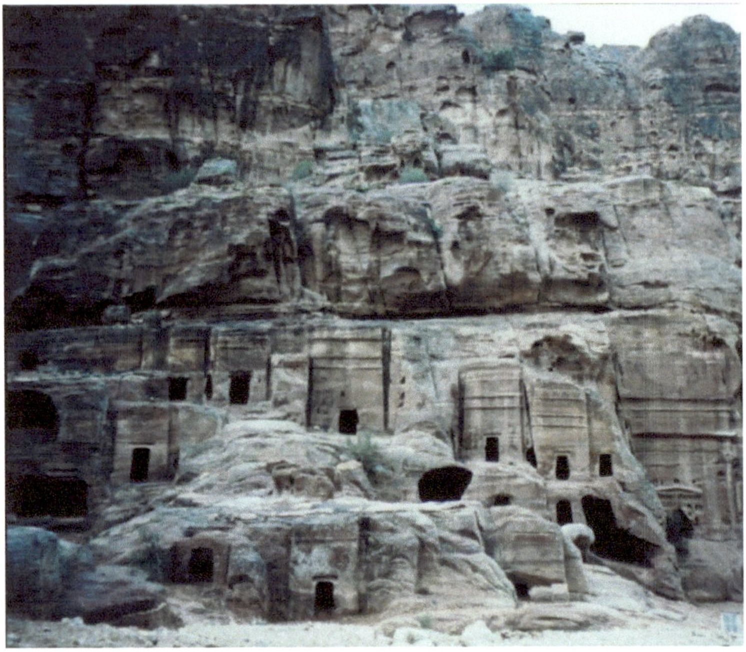

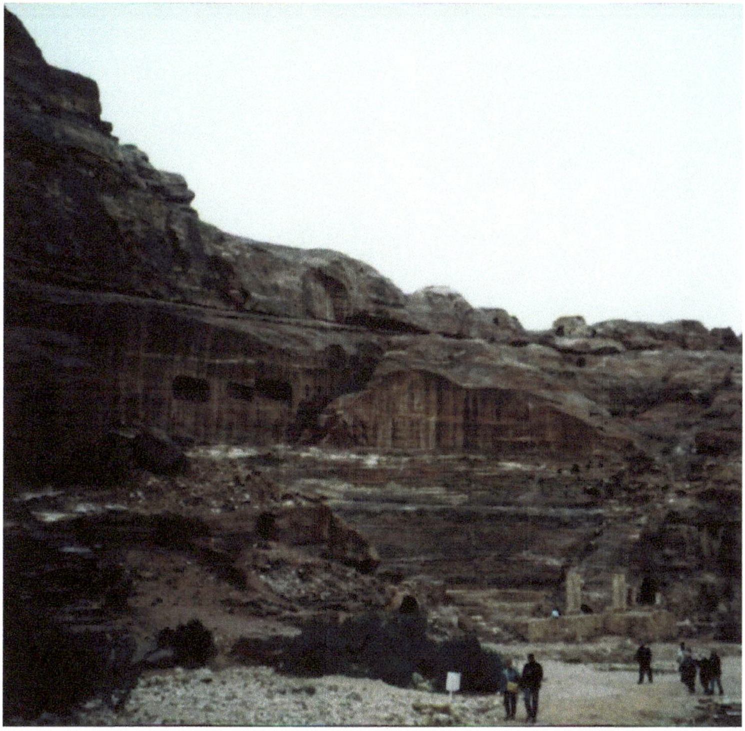

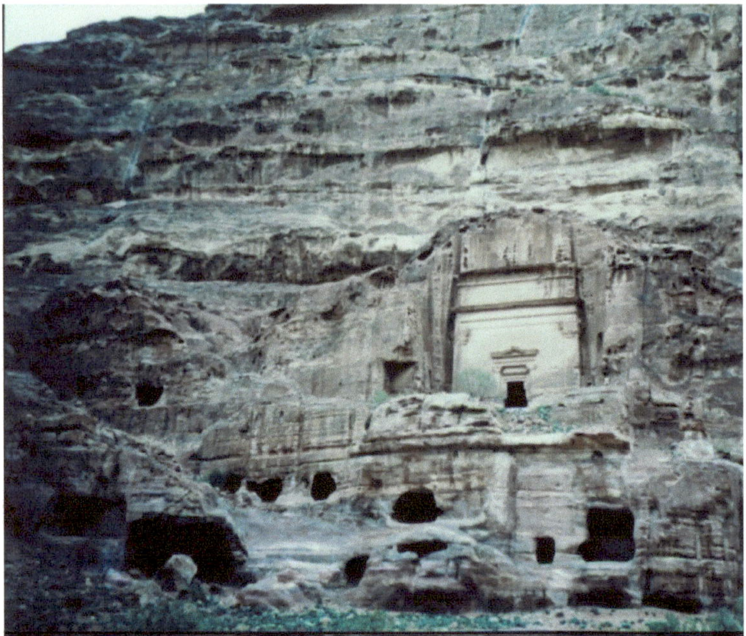

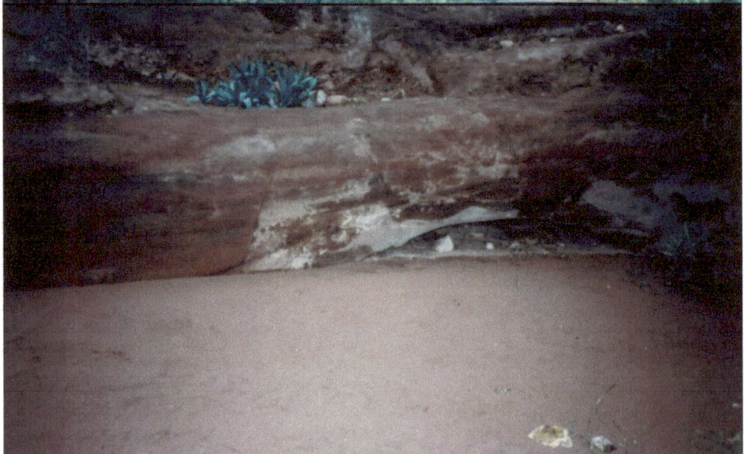

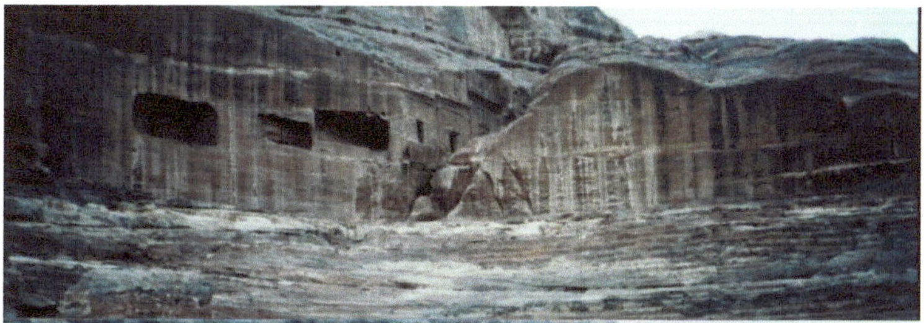

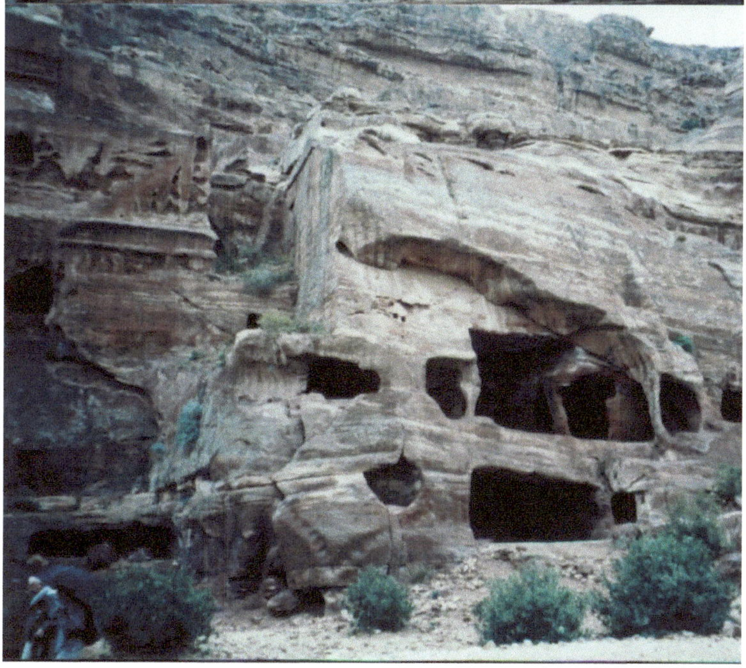

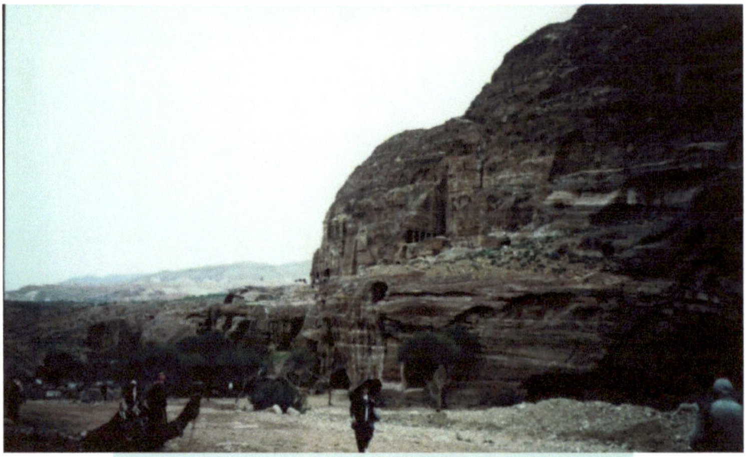

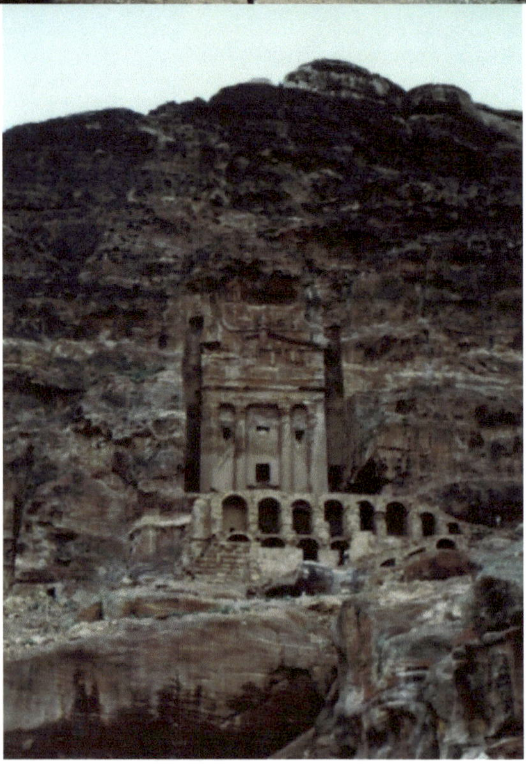

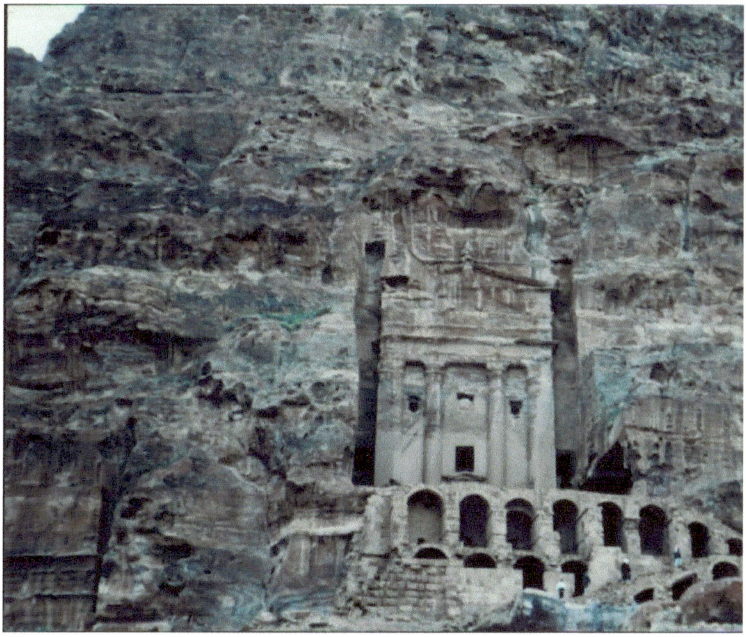

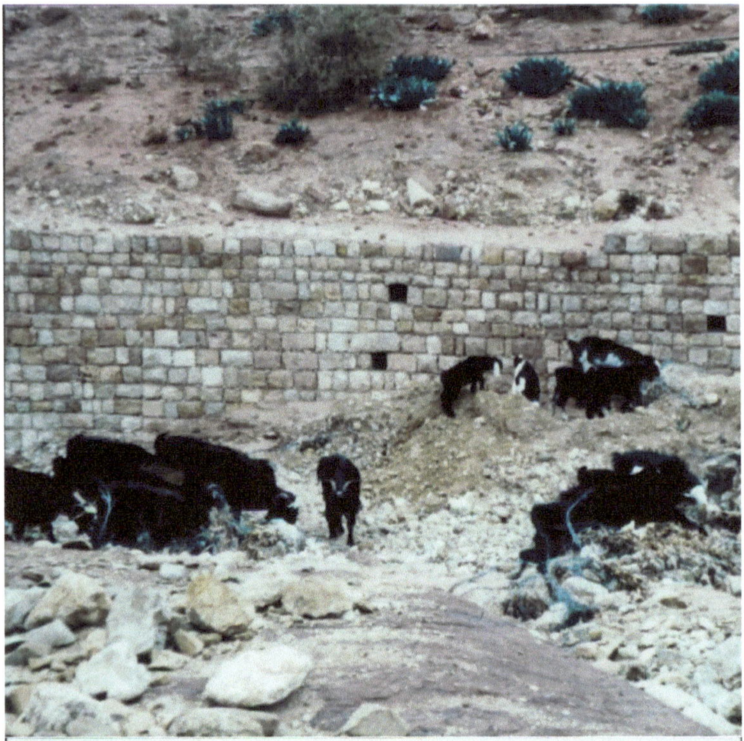
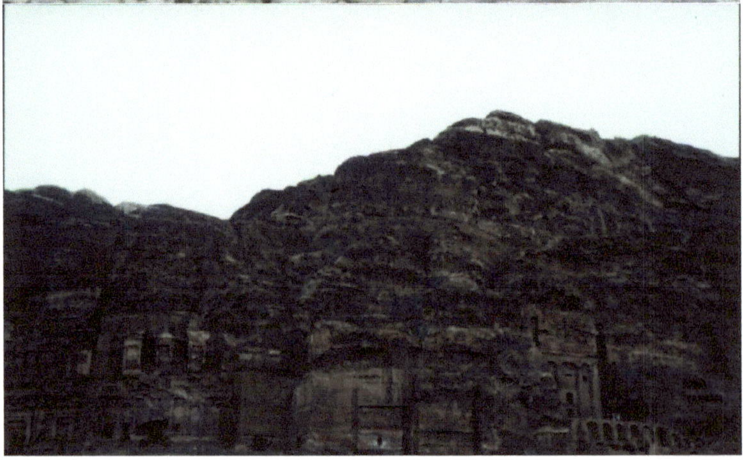

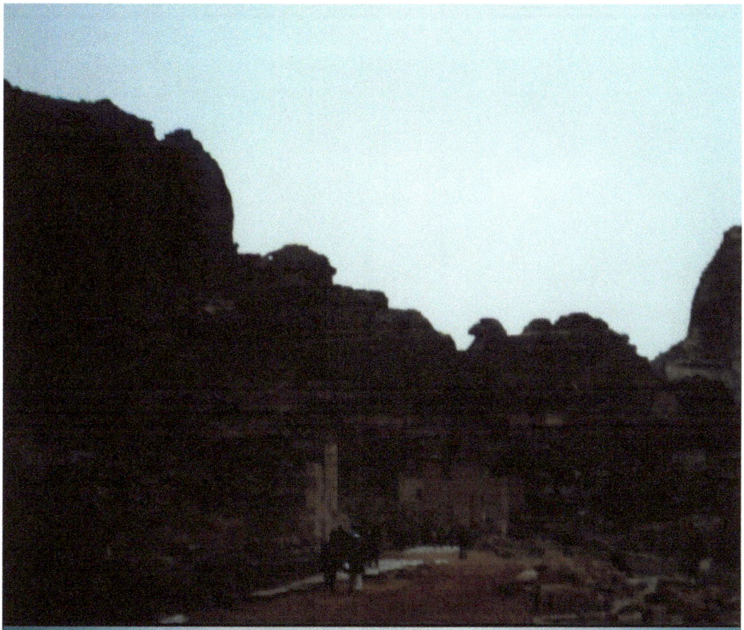

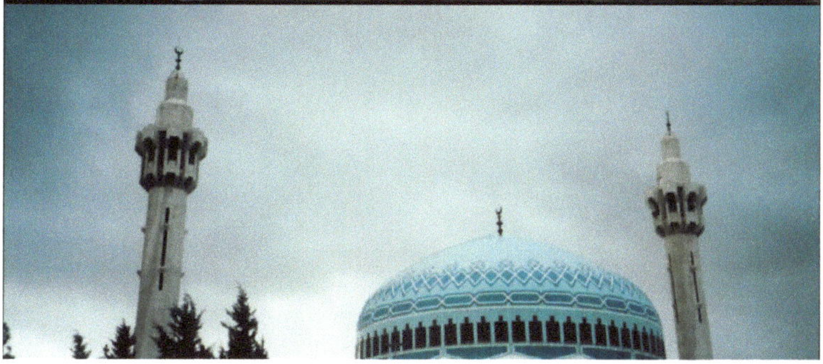

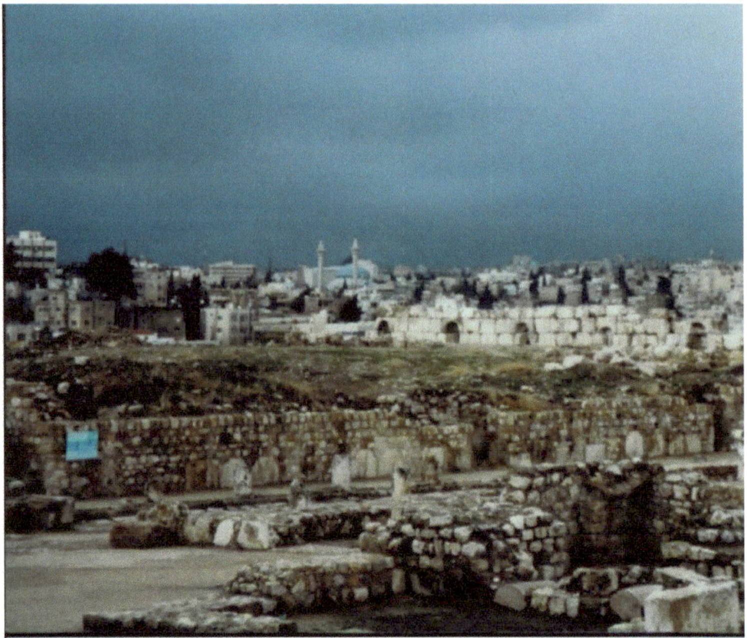

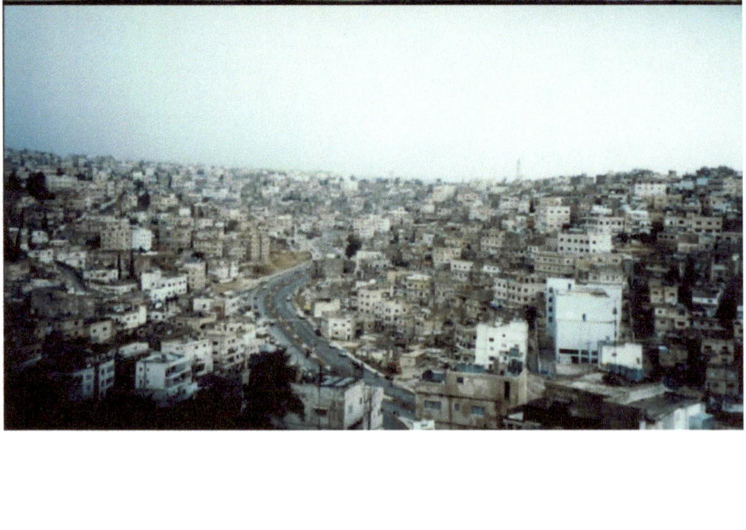

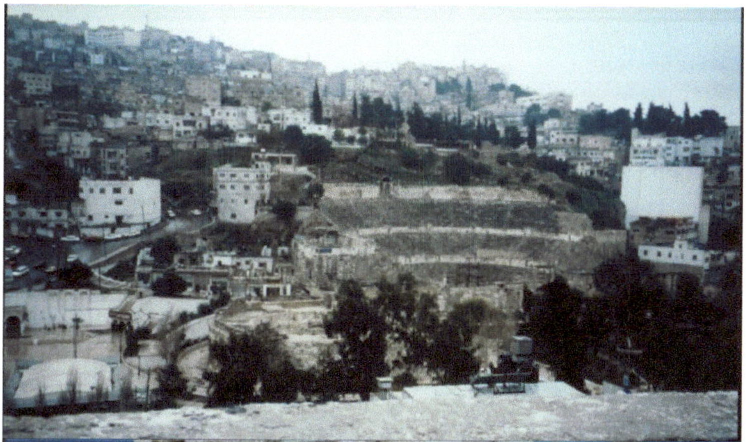

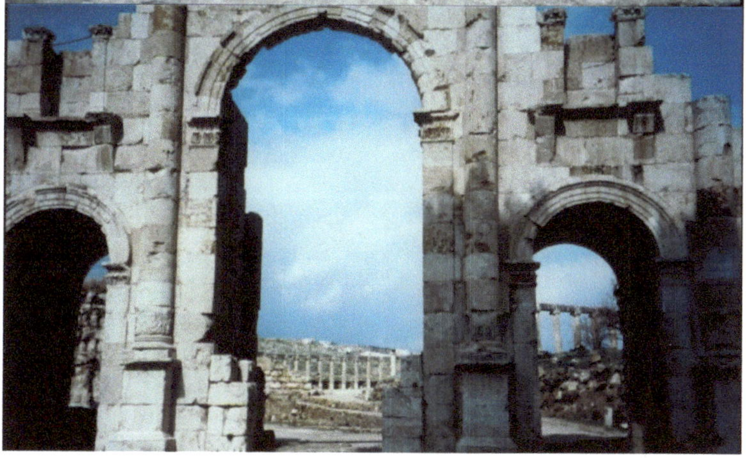

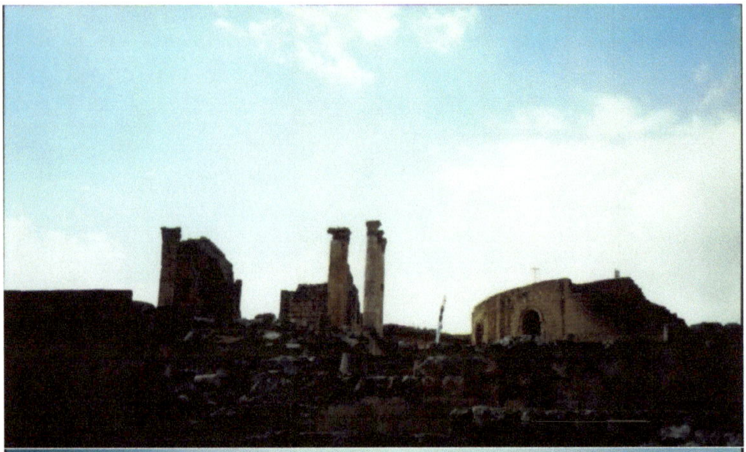

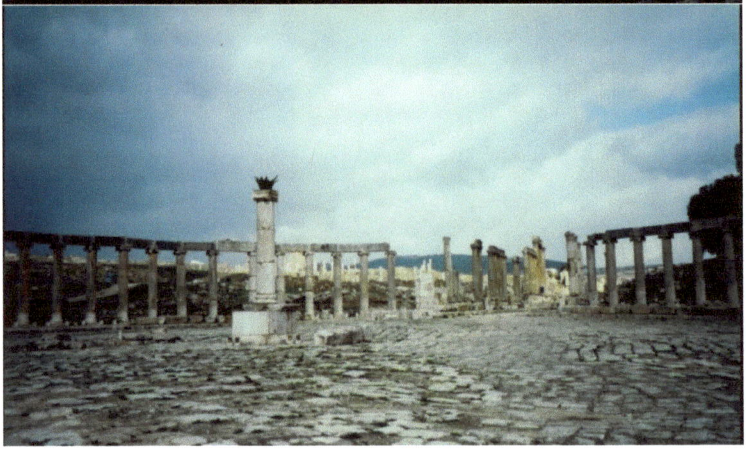

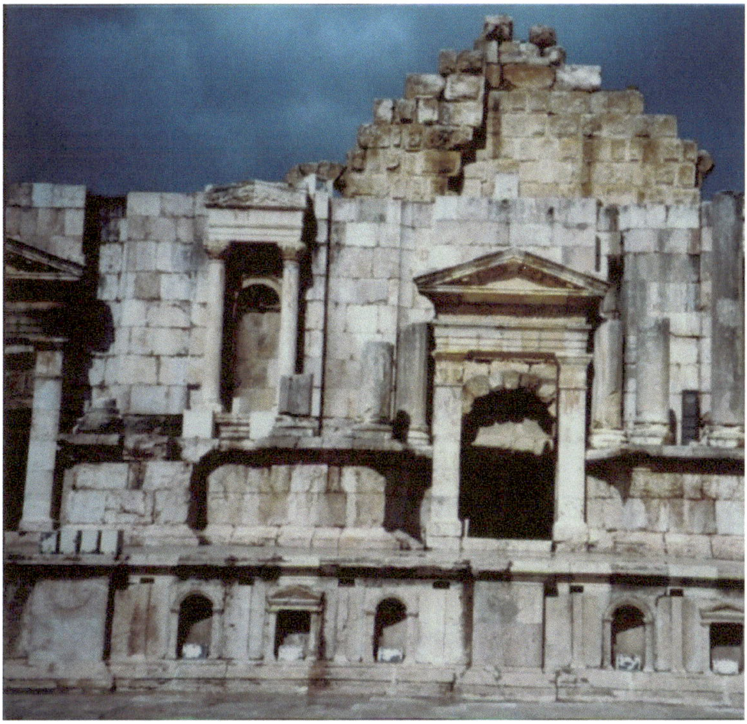

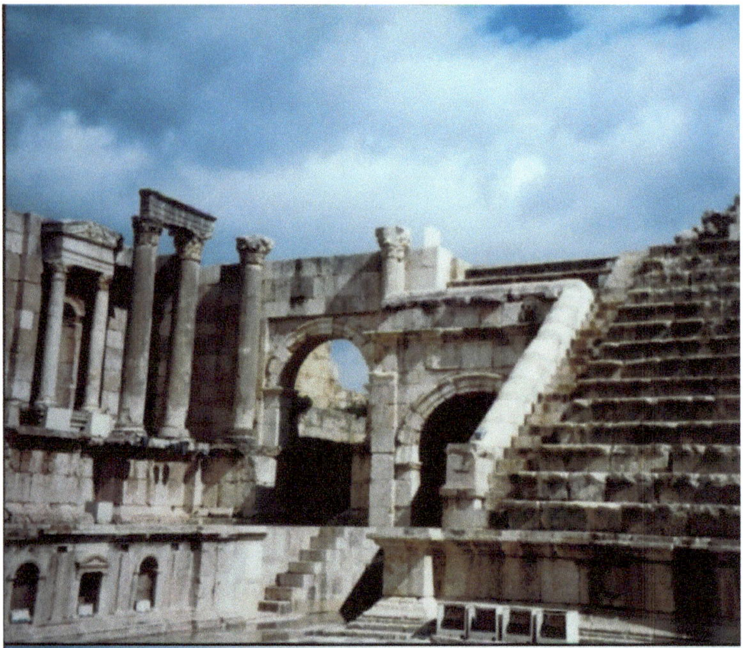

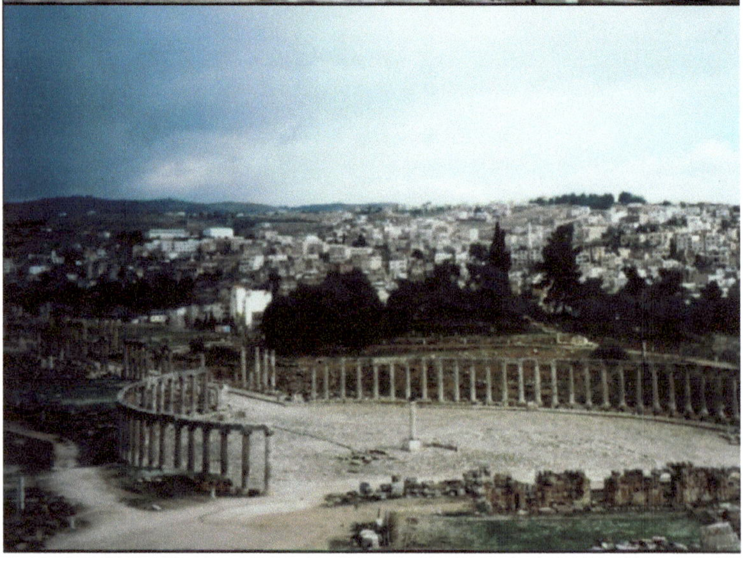

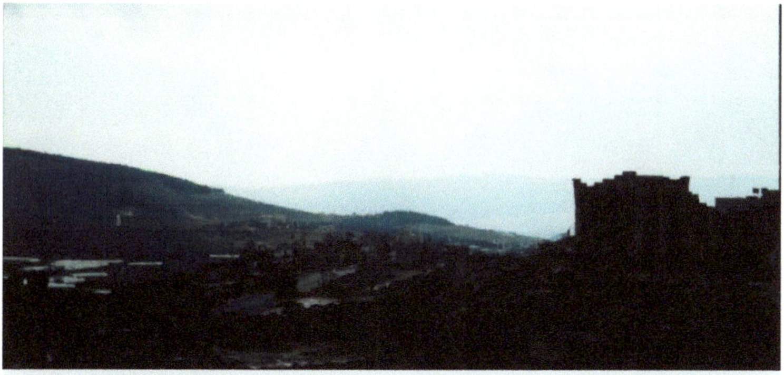

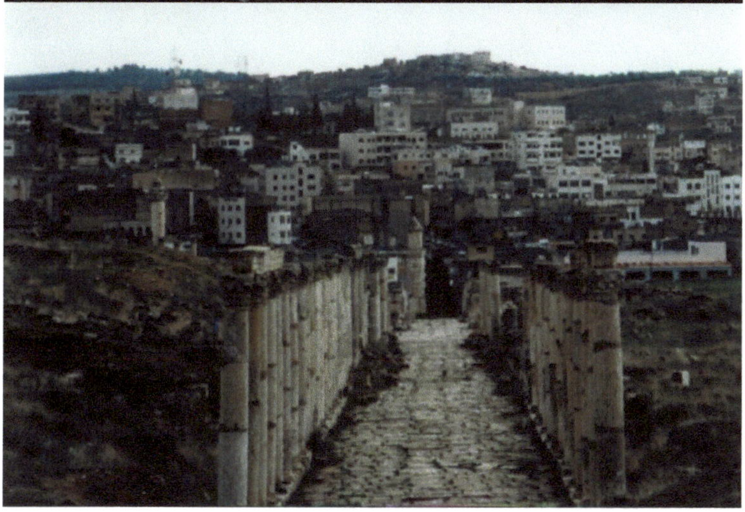

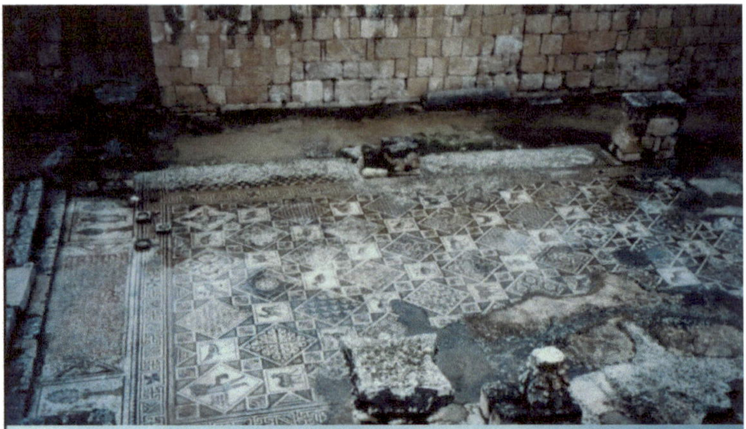
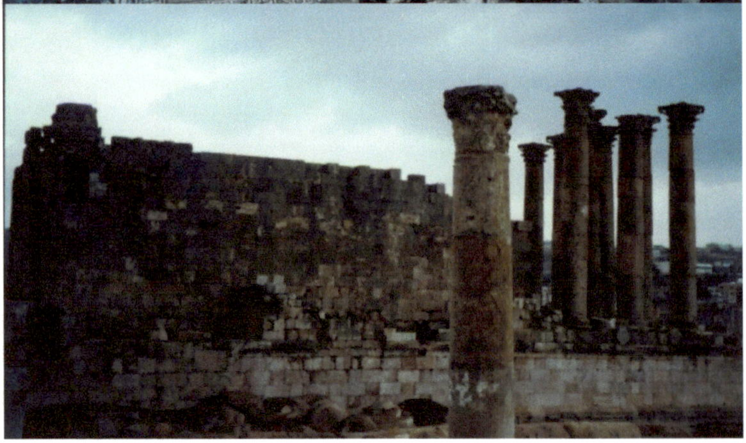

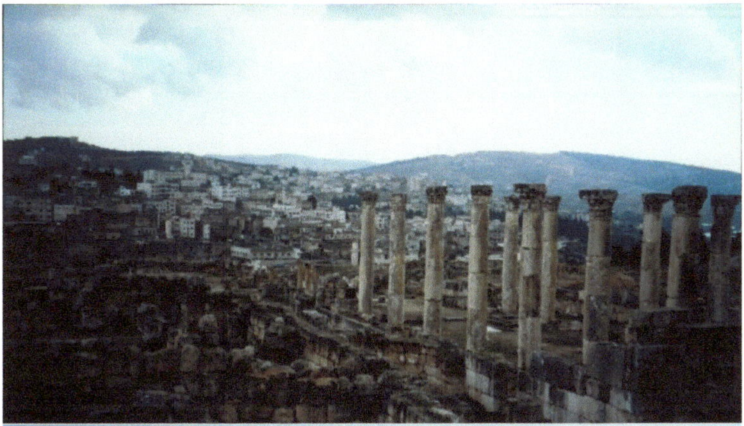

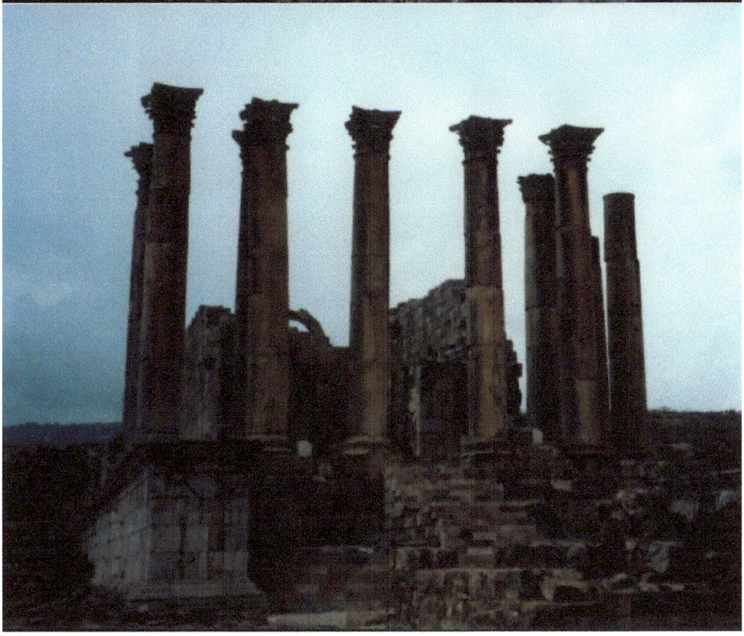

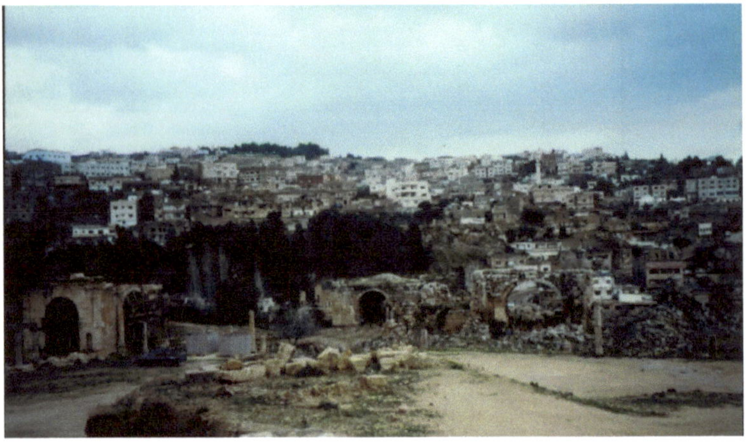

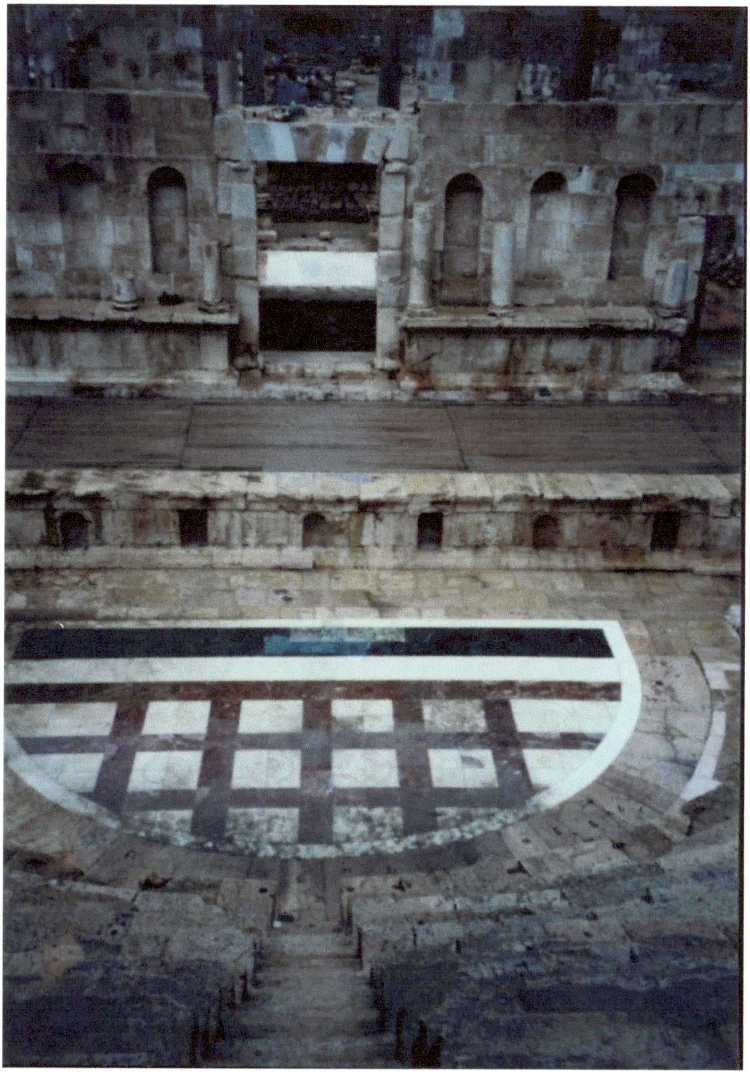

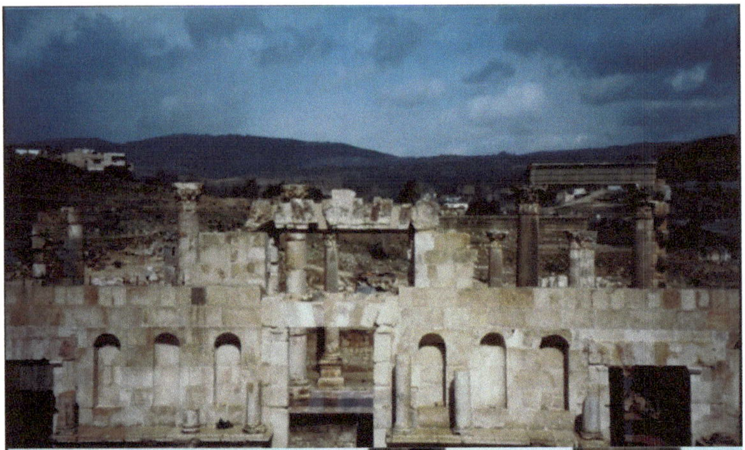

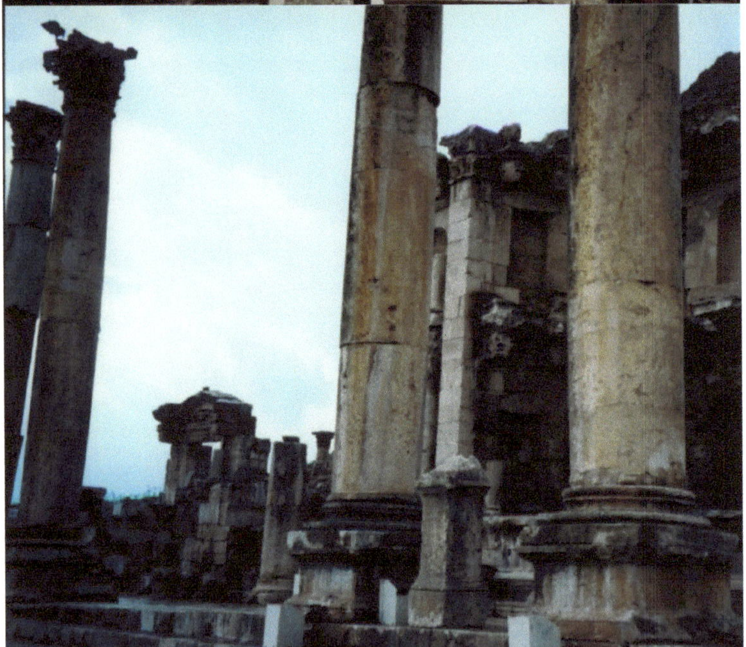

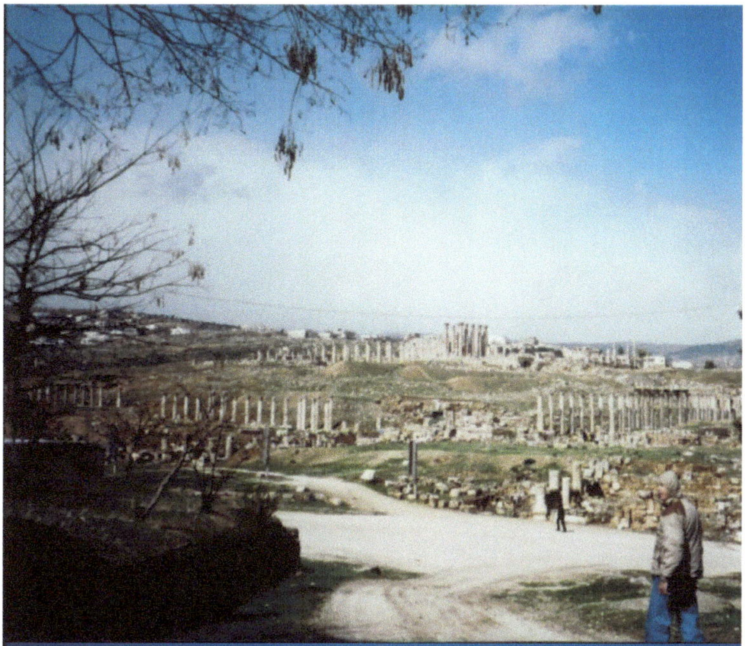

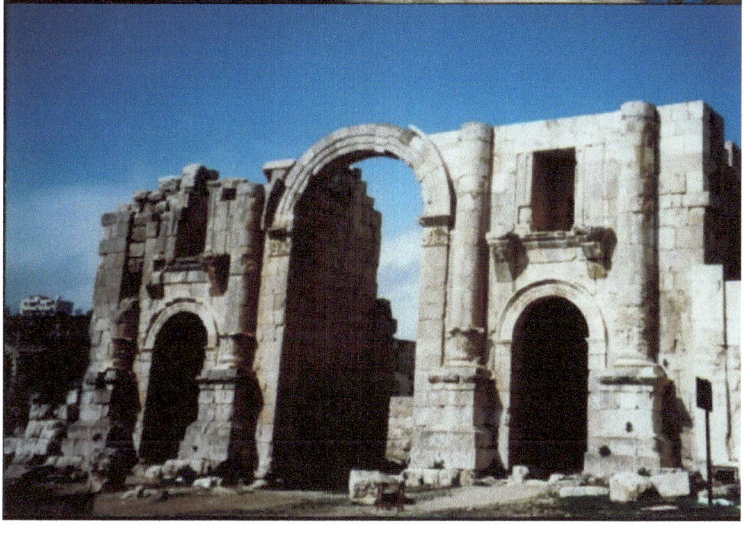

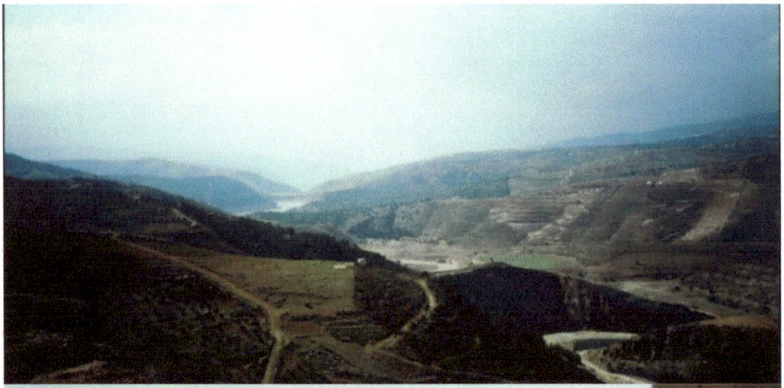

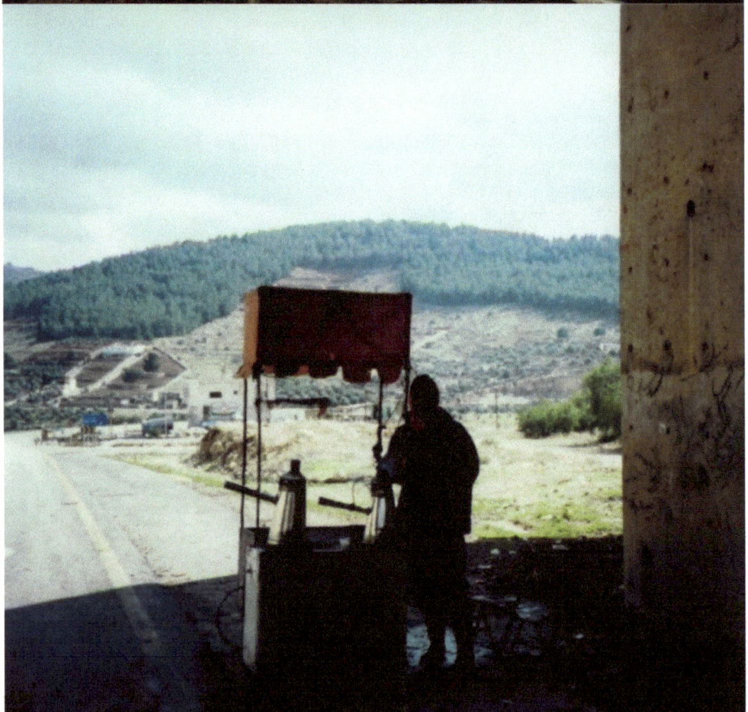

www.ingramcontent.com/pod-product-compliance
Lightning Source LLC
Chambersburg PA
CBHW041609180526
45159CB00002BC/792
* 9 7 8 1 5 1 4 8 6 5 0 9 5 *